SPOTLIGHT ON SPACE SCIENCE

# JOURNEY TO EARTH

## BETSY OATES

**PowerKiDS** press.

New York

Published in 2015 by The Rosen Publishing Group, Inc.
29 East 21st Street, New York, NY 10010

First Edition

Editor: Susan Meyer
Book Design: Kris Everson

Photo Credits: Cover (main) Jan Erik Paulsen/NASA; cover (planet Earth) NASA/JPL; p. 5 NASA/GSFC/Suomi NPP; p. 7 NASA, ESA, M. Robberto (Space Telescope Science Institute/ESA) and the Hubble Space Telescope Orion Treasury Project Team; pp. 9, 15 NASA; p. 11 NASA/Solar Dynamics Observatory; p. 13 John Anderson/iStock/Thinkstock.com; p. 14 Shutterstock.com; p. 17 curraheeshutter/iStock/Thinkstock.com; p. 19 Dtamarack/iStock/Thinkstock.com; p. 21 TimHesterPhotography/iStock/Thinkstock.com; p. 23 NASA/JSC; p. 25 ziggy_mars/iStock/Thinkstock.com; p. 26 hecke61/Shutterstock.com; p. 27 defun/iStock/Thinkstock.com; p. 29 NASA/Ames/JPL-Caltech.

Library of Congress Cataloging-in-Publication Data

Oates, Betsy.
Journey to Earth / by Betsy Oates.
p. cm. — (Spotlight on space science)
Includes index.
ISBN 978-1-4994-0368-8 (pbk.)
ISBN 978-1-4994-0397-8 (6-pack)
ISBN 978-1-4994-0412-8 (library binding)
1. Earth (Planet) — Juvenile literature. I. Title.
QB631.4 O184 2015
525—d23

Manufactured in the United States of America

CPSIA Compliance Information: Batch #CW15PK: For Further Information contact Rosen Publishing, New York, New York at 1-800-237-9932

# CONTENTS

# A PLANET TO CALL HOME

## CHAPTER 1

A visitor from outer space approaching Earth, with its blue waters, green and brown land masses, and white, cloudy **atmosphere**, would view a swirl of color against the blackness of space.

Upon landing, that visitor would find a world unlike any of the other seven **planets** or millions of other objects that orbit our Sun. Like other worlds in our **solar system**, Earth has a mixture of chemicals that produce landforms, an atmosphere, weather patterns, and various kinds of liquids and gases. But nowhere else in the solar system do all these **elements** come together to produce the incredible variety of features we have on Earth.

Earth is also the only world in our solar system where, so far, any form of life is known to exist. And even more amazingly, Earth is the only planet we know of in the **universe**, again, so far,

**where the kind of intelligent life exists that makes it possible for you to be reading this book!**

*Here is the planet Earth as seen from the top, looking down on the North Pole.*

# HOW A SOLAR SYSTEM FORMS

## CHAPTER 2

Earth and the other planets in the solar system were created when our Sun formed about 4.5 billion years ago.

Before the solar system came into being, there was a huge cloud of gas and dust in space. Over time, the cloud collapsed on itself. Most of the gas and dust formed a massive spinning sphere, or ball. As the sphere spun in space, a disk formed around the sphere from the remaining gas and dust. As all this matter rotated, the sphere pulled in more gas and dust, adding to its size, weight, and **gravity**. The pressure of all the material pressing onto the center of the sphere caused the center to get hotter and hotter. Finally, the temperature inside the sphere got so hot that the sphere ignited to become a new star. That star was our Sun!

Leftover gas and dust continued to spin in a disk around the Sun. Over time, this matter clumped together to form eight planets, including our Earth, the planets' moons, and smaller objects such as **dwarf planets** and **asteroids**.

*This photo, taken by the Hubble Space Telescope, shows the Orion Nebula. Inside this mass of gas and dust, new stars are forming. Each of these stars has the potential to form its own solar system, like our own.*

# THE EIGHT PLANETS

## CHAPTER 3

For around 4.5 billion years, the planets in our solar system have been orbiting the Sun, each taking its own path, or orbit, around our star.

Five of the solar system's planets, Mercury, Venus, Mars, Jupiter, and Saturn, can be seen in the sky with the naked eye, so they were known about from earliest times.

In March 1781, British astronomer Sir William Herschel observed Uranus for the first time. At first, he thought he'd seen a **comet**. In September 1846, German astronomer Johann Gottfried Galle discovered Neptune.

Then, in 1930, American astronomer Clyde Tombaugh discovered a tiny, distant planet, which was named Pluto. For decades, therefore, our solar system was home to nine planets. In 2007, however, the International Astronomical

Union reclassified Pluto as a dwarf planet because of its small size. Also, Pluto does not have the gravitational power to "sweep up" all the objects close to it and pull them into its orbit, like the eight larger "true" planets.

*In this, not to scale, artist's representation, Earth can be seen as the third planet from the Sun.*

# THE POWER OF THE SUN

## CHAPTER 4

Earth continually orbits the Sun at an average distance of about 93 million miles (150 million km) away. That distance is very important for our planet because it means we are in a zone that scientists sometimes call "the Goldilocks Zone."

The Goldilocks Zone gets its name because at this distance from the Sun, it is neither too hot nor too cold. The "just right" temperatures and conditions inside the zone mean Earth is able to support liquid water, which is essential for living things to develop and stay alive.

As a star, our Sun is not particularly special, and it has no unusual features. Like the billions of other stars in the Milky Way, it is just a burning ball of hydrogen and helium gases. It's very easy, in fact, to take the Sun's energy for granted.

Without the Sun's light and heat, however, we could not exist on our home planet.

The Sun is a massive ball of energy. Sometimes this energy causes huge "arms" of solar plasma to erupt from its surface.

# ORBIT AND ROTATION

CHAPTER 5

We call the time period that it takes a planet to make one full orbit of the Sun a year. Earth orbits the Sun once every 365 days, so a year on Earth is 365 days.

To make one full orbit of the Sun, Earth travels a distance of 584 million miles (940 million km). It is moving through space at an average speed of 66,622 miles per hour (107,218 km/h).

While Earth is orbiting the Sun, it's also spinning, or rotating, on its **axis**. It makes one full rotation every 24 hours.

The Earth doesn't spin completely upright because its axis is slightly tilted at 23.5 degrees. As the planet moves around the Sun, this tilt causes Earth to have different seasons.When the planet's northern **hemisphere** is tilted towards the Sun, the north has summer and the south has winter. When the southern hemisphere tilts towards the Sun, the south has summer and the north has winter.

When it is winter in New York City in the northern hemisphere, it's summer in Santiago, Chile, in the southern hemisphere.

# EARTH'S MOON

## CHAPTER 6

Traveling through space at an average distance of about 238,855 miles (384,400 km) from Earth is the Moon. As Earth orbits the Sun, the Moon is orbiting Earth. It makes one full orbit of our planet every 27.3 days.

Over the years there have been many theories as to how the Moon formed. One theory was that the Moon formed alongside the Earth from material left over from the birth of the Sun. Today, most

Earth

Mars-sized impactor planet

This artwork shows how rock from Eart may have formed the Moon following a impact with another planet.

scientists believe a planet, or some other space body the size of Mars, crashed into Earth soon after it formed. Superheated chunks of Earth and the impactor planet flew out into space. Over time this debris clumped together to form the Moon, which has continued to orbit Earth to this day.

Our Moon has one very important claim to fame. Its rocky, dusty surface is the only place in the universe, other than Earth, where a human has ever stood!

*This photo of Earth from the Moon was taken in 1969 by the Apollo 11 mission. The spacecraft in the photo is the Eagle Lander.*

# FROM CORE TO CRUST

## CHAPTER 7

Earth is made up of three layers called the crust, the mantle, and the core. Where there is land, Earth's rocky crust is 15 to 35 miles (24 to 56 km) thick. Beneath the planet's oceans, the crust is just 3 to 5 miles (4.8 to 8 km) thick.

Below the crust is the mantle. The upper layer of the mantle is formed from rock. Beneath this rigid upper layer, however, it is so hot that rock actually melts and forms thick, oozing, **molten** rock.

Deep inside the Earth is the core. The outer layer of the core is made of molten iron and nickel. Here, temperatures reach about 8,000°F (4,400°C). The inner core is a solid mass of metal with a temperature of around 9,000°F (5,000°C). That's as hot as the surface of the Sun.

*Even the deepest oil wells still only skim the surface.*
*The deepest well on Earth is over 7 miles (11 km)*
*deep—still less than halfway through the Earth's crust*
*at its thinnest point.*

# PLATE TECTONICS
## CHAPTER 8

Throughout the history of our planet, constant movements in the Earth's crust and flows of **magma** that burst onto the Earth's surface have been changing and shaping the look of our planet.

Earth's crust is broken into large pieces, called tectonic plates, that fit together like a giant jigsaw puzzle.The tectonic plates are constantly moving, which squeezes and stretches the rocks that make up the crust. One way that we see the results of these movements is when we look at ancient mountains. Often, the mountains will have formed when layers of rock rose up, buckling and folding over each other, on either side of a huge crack that appeared in the Earth's crust.

Sometimes, as the Earth's crust moves and cracks it allows magma from inside the mantle to come to the surface.The lava flows over the ground.

Then it cools and hardens, forming layers of new rock, and creating a new landscape.

*When volcanoes erupt, hot lava flows, changing the landscape and building new rocks.*

# HIGH MOUNTAINS AND DEEP CANYONS

CHAPTER 9

Like the other terrestrial planets in the solar system, Earth's surface is covered in a wide variety of rocky features including mountains, volcanoes, and **canyons**.

The tallest mountain on Earth is Mount Everest. Standing nearly 5.5 miles (8.8 km) high, Earth's record-breaking mountain is part of the Himalayas **mountain range** on the border of China and Nepal, in Asia.

At 6.3 miles (10.2 km) high, the inactive volcano, Mauna Kea, which forms part of the island of Hawaii, is actually taller than Mount Everest. Only the top 2.6 miles (4.2 km) of this giant is above **sea level**, however, and the heights of mountains are always officially measured above sea level.

Earth's longest **mountain chain** is the Andes. The mountains stretch along the west coast of

South America for about 5,500 miles (8,800 km). The mountain chain was formed about 70 million years ago by the collision of two of Earth's tectonic plates.

*The Himalaya Mountains in South Asia contain the highest mountain in the world, Mount Everest. They were formed by two tectonic plates pushing together.*

# A BLANKET OF PROTECTIVE GASES
## CHAPTER 10

Earth's atmosphere is a protective blanket of gases that surround our planet at heights up to 75 miles (120 km) above the planet's surface.

The atmosphere is made up of 78 percent nitrogen, 21 percent oxygen, and 1 percent other gases.

By day, Earth's atmosphere stops the planet from becoming too hot. At night, the layer of gases stores daytime heat, keeping the planet warm. This stored heat prevents temperatures from dropping as they do on the planet Mercury, which has no atmosphere. At night, with no stored heat to warm the planet, temperatures on Mercury plummet to −280°F (−173°C)!

Earth's atmosphere also absorbs dangerous rays from the Sun and protects our world from objects such as small meteoroids and asteroids that are on a collision course with Earth. As rocky space objects head for our planet, they enter the protective atmosphere and are burned up or broken into smaller pieces that rarely cause damage when they hit Earth's surface.

*The sky appears black outside of Earth's atmosphere.*

# WATER, WATER EVERYWHERE
## CHAPTER 11

You may have heard people describe our planet as "the blue planet." This is because about 70 percent of Earth's surface is covered with water, and from space, the planet looks blue.

We are probably most familiar with water in its liquid state, but it also exists as a solid, when frozen, or as a gas called water vapor, when it evaporates. Liquid water is found on Earth in the oceans, in lakes, in rivers and streams, and even underground. Water as solid ice exists on mountain tops, in **glaciers**, and in the polar ice caps, which are huge sheets of ice at the North and South Poles. Water vapor is in the air all around us.

Water plays a huge role in the life of our planet. Over half of the **species** of animals, plants, and other life forms that inhabit our planet live in water. And of those species that do not live in water, all of them require water in some form in order to stay alive.

*Seventy-one percent of Earth is covered in water, but only 3 percent of that is freshwater. This photo shows Victoria Falls, one of the largest waterfalls in the world.*

# THRIVING LIFE

## CHAPTER 12

Life is one of the things that makes Earth unique among all the planets in our solar system.

Today astronomers and other scientists are closer than they have ever been to figuring out if there is any chance that even the smallest, simplest

Even in the very coldest oceans on Earth, life exists!

**organisms** may ever have existed in other parts of the solar system. Even if such evidence turns up, however, we can be pretty sure that no other world orbiting our Sun has ever had the incredible variety and complexity of life forms that we enjoy on Earth.

Earth is home to microscopic bacteria that live inside our bodies and in parts of the Earth that are so hot or cold as to seem uninhabitable. It is also home to mammals, birds, reptiles, insects, spiders, and about half a million different types of plants. Scientists are not in complete agreement about how many different kinds of life are on Earth today. Some estimate, however, that there may be as many as 8.7 million entirely different species!

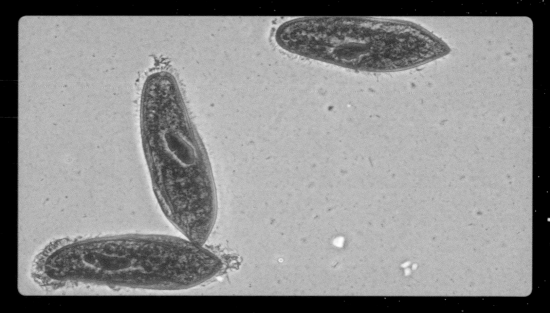

*The earliest organisms were made up of a single cell, like these paramecium. Later organisms became much more complex. Humans, for example, are made up of many trillions of cells.*

# IS ANYONE OUT THERE?
## CHAPTER 13

For centuries, humans have wanted to know if life exists, and in particular, intelligent life, in other parts of the universe. Could there be another Earthlike planet out there? Is it possible that we are not alone?

While astronomers have been able to observe stars beyond our solar system for centuries, it was too difficult to see if there were planets orbiting those stars.

In March 2009, the Kepler space observatory, which carries a powerful telescope, was launched. Kepler's mission is to study part of the Milky Way and look for exoplanets. In particular, the mission is hoping to discover planets that are orbiting their stars in the Goldilocks Zone, where there is liquid water and temperatures are neither too hot nor too cold and a planet could support life!

By the end of 2014, Kepler scientists had confirmed the discovery of nearly 1,000 planets and more than 4,000 objects that might be planets. While confirmation that another Earth exists is yet to come, perhaps one day soon we will get an answer to the question: Are we alone?

*The Kepler telescope uses a photometer to detect light from far-off stars and determine if any exoplanets*

# GLOSSARY

**asteroid:** A small, rocky, planet-like body in space that circles the Sun.

**atmosphere:** The gases that surround Earth.

**axis:** An imaginary line through the center of an object, around which the object rotates.

**canyon:** A deep valley with steep sides.

**comet:** A body in space made up of dust, gas, and ice that orbits the sun. It sometimes develops a bright, long tail.

**dwarf planet:** A large body in space that orbits the sun, but isn't large enough to be called a planet.

**element:** A part of something.

**glacier:** A large body of ice that moves slowly down a valley or land surface, carrying loose rock and other matter.

**gravity:** The attraction of the mass of a body in space for other bodies nearby.

**hemisphere:** A half of Earth.

**magma:** Rock that has become liquid through extreme heat.

**molten:** Turned to liquid by heat.

**mountain chain:** A group of mountain ranges.

**mountain range:** A large group of mountains close together.

**organism:** A living thing.

**planet:** A large body in space that has its own motion around the Sun or another star.

**sea level:** The level directly at the surface of the sea, halfway between high and low tides.

**solar system:** The Sun and the space bodies that move around it, including the planets and their moons.

**species:** A group of living things that are all the same kind.

**universe:** Everything that exists.

# FOR MORE INFORMATION

## BOOKS

Chancellor, Deborah. *Planet Earth*. New York, NY: Kingfisher, 2014.

Murrie, Matthew, and Steve Murrie. *Up Close!* New York, NY: Scholastic, 2010.

Ride, Sally, and Tam E. Shaughnessy. *Mission Planet Earth: Our World and Its Climate—and How Humans Are Changing Them*. New York, NY: Flash Point/Roaring Brook, 2009.

## WEBSITES

Due to the changing nature of Internet links, PowerKids Press has developed an online list of websites related to the subject of this book. This site is updated regularly. Please use this link to access the list: www.powerkidslinks.com/soss/earth

# INDEX